Contents

What Does It Take to Be a Bird?	4
Bird Habitats	6
Waterbirds	8
Freshwater Habitats	10
Birdwatching	12
Saltwater Habitats	14
The Shearwater's Year	16
Waterbird Alphabet	18
Glossary	22
Index	23
Discussion Starters	24

Features

What is *a habitat*? Where did this word come from? Find out on page 7.

Do you know that most waterbirds have waterproof feathers? Learn how birds keep feathers waterproof on page 11.

Lots of people enjoy birdwatching. Find out what to look for and how to identify birds in **Birdwatching** on page 12.

Long-distance travellers are in the news! Read about the shearwater's amazing journey in **Millions Fly North** on page 17.

What happens at nesting time?
Visit **www.infosteps.co.uk**
for more about BIRDS.

What Does It Take to Be a Bird?

About 6,000 million people live on Earth. Do you know that more than 100,000 million birds live on our planet too? Birds come in many sizes and colours. They do things in many different ways. Most birds are built for flying. However, some birds have lost their ability to fly. All birds have certain things in common.

All birds:
- have feathers,
- have a beak,
- have two wings,
- have two legs,
- have one or more songs or calls,
- have warm blood,
- lay eggs.

FLIGHT CONTROL
Tail feathers help steer and brake.

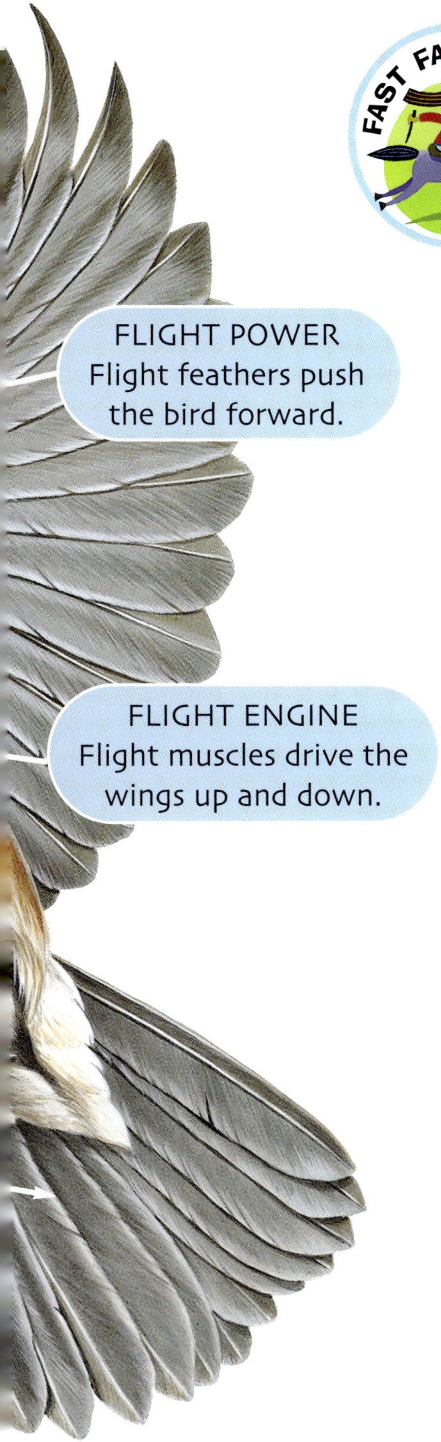

Catching the Wind

FLIGHT POWER
Flight feathers push the bird forward.

FLIGHT ENGINE
Flight muscles drive the wings up and down.

Some birds ride columns of warm air called **thermals**.

Some birds such as gulls get a free ride on **updrafts**.

Strong winds blow over the ocean. These winds are weaker down by the water and stronger high in the sky. Birds use these different wind strengths when they fly.

Bird Habitats

Birds live in many different places. They are suited to life in many **habitats**, including deserts, forests, rainforests, grasslands, coastlines and **wetlands**. In these habitats birds find food, make nests, lay eggs and raise their young.

We can tell a lot about a bird's habitat and what it eats by looking at its beak, feet and legs.

The bald eagle is a raptor, or bird of prey.

What happens at nesting time?

Visit **www.infosteps.co.uk** for more about BIRDS.

WORD BUILDER

A *habitat* is a place where a plant or an animal lives. It comes from the Latin word *habitare*, which means "to live in".

Curved beak for tearing flesh

Talons for gripping prey

Waterbirds

Nearly two-thirds of Earth's surface is covered in water, so it is not surprising that many birds are waterbirds. They live by the oceans or near lakes, rivers, ponds and streams.

Waterbirds are suited to their watery habitats. Some have long legs for wading in water. Some have webbed feet to help them swim well. Many waterbirds have unusual beaks, or bills, that are specially shaped for getting food.

The brown pelican uses its bill like a net to scoop up fish swimming near the surface.

When feeding, a flamingo drags its hooked beak through the water. It scoops up muddy water containing small shellfish and insects.

Freshwater Habitats

Swamps, rivers, lakes and ponds are all freshwater habitats. Many kinds of birds live in these places.

In many parts of the world **wetlands** are in danger from **pollution** or from being drained so people can use the land.

When a wetland becomes polluted birds living there are forced to find a new home.

FAST FACTS

Most waterbirds have waterproof feathers. When a waterbird **preens** it presses its bill on a gland at the base of its tail and a special oil comes out. The bird then rubs its oily bill on its feathers. Then when the bird gets wet the water rolls off its feathers.

Birdwatching

Many people enjoy watching and identifying birds. A good place to start birdwatching is at a park, pond or lake.

To identify birds notice the differences between:

- Wing markings
- Eye markings
- Beaks
- Legs and feet

Key to Waterbirds

Use this key to identify the waterbirds.

Mallard duck

White swan

Shoveller duck

Canada goose

Seagull

Black swan

Saltwater Habitats

Oceans and seas surround Earth's land. Wherever there is sea water there are places that attract birds. Birds flock to these coastal habitats to feed and nest.

Some seabirds scoop fish from the water's surface. Others dive to catch fish swimming below the surface. Some seabirds search the shorelines for shellfish and crabs. They all have eyes, beaks, legs, feet and wings that help them in their search for food.

FAST FACTS

Many seabirds nest in colonies of thousands of birds. The birds return to the same colony each year to nest. In many places colonies are protected.

The Shearwater's Year

Many seabirds **migrate** long distances during their lifetime. Each winter a bird called the short-tailed shearwater flies from its nesting grounds in Australia to the rich feeding area of the Bering Sea, between northeast Asia and Alaska. Short-tailed shearwaters come to shore only when it is nesting time.

June, July, August
The birds feed in the Bering Sea.

September
After a long flight the birds return to their nesting islands off the southeast coast of Australia.

October, November
The birds make nests, pair up and return to sea to feed. Females lay one egg in November.

IN THE NEWS

Saturday, May 2

Millions Fly North

Yesterday birdwatchers reported flocks of as many as 250,000 short-tailed shearwaters flying overhead every hour. Millions of these birds are leaving their Australian nesting grounds for a long flight north. The shearwaters will spend several weeks flying to their winter home off the coast of Alaska. In September they will fly back to Australia to build their nests and raise their chicks. Altogether these amazing birds will have flown over 30,500 kilometres.

December, January
Parents take turns staying with their egg until it hatches in January.

February, March
Chicks grow quickly. Parents take turns bringing food to their chick once every three days.

April, May
Chicks are now fully grown. The birds leave their nesting grounds and migrate to the Bering Sea.

Waterbird Alphabet

Albatross
A huge seabird with a wingspan of 1.3 metres to 3 metres, it flies over oceans searching for food.

A

B

Bittern
A waterbird that is good at camouflage, it hides by lifting its head and swaying with the reeds.

Cormorant
The cormorant catches fish underwater. Its feathers are not waterproof, so it often spreads its wings to dry.

C

D

Dabchick
A dabchick spends most of its life on the water, and it even builds floating nests.

Emperor Penguin
The largest member of the penguin family at 1.2 metres tall, the emperor penguin cannot fly and lives in the Antarctic.

E

FAST FACTS

Frigate Bird
A large bird from the tropics, the male inflates his red throat pouch so the female can see him from the air.

Gannet
This large seabird has excellent eyesight and dives into the sea from amazing heights.

Heron
Most herons have long necks and powerful beaks designed for stabbing prey such as fish and frogs.

Ibis
The ibis is a wading bird that lives in wetland colonies of thousands of birds.

Jacana
This bird is sometimes called a "lily trotter". It has long legs and long toes for wading and running across lily pads.

Kittiwake
A gull that comes ashore only to nest, it spends most of its life at sea. Its name is from its cry of *kitty-wake*.

Loon
Also called a "diver", the loon lives by many lakes and ponds in Canada and near the Arctic Circle. Its haunting cry can be heard for long distances.

Mallard
The female's feathers are mostly brown. The male has bright blue-green feathers on its head and wings.

Osprey
Often called a fish hawk or fish killer, the osprey plunges feet-first into the water and grabs fish with its talons.

Pelican
A sea and freshwater bird, the pelican has a huge beak and throat pouch. Pelicans are brown or black and white.

Rail
The rail has long legs and toes suited to its wetland habitat. It has small wings and does not fly well.

Stork
A long-necked, long-legged wading bird, the stork builds huge nests from piles of branches and twigs.

Tern
The tern is a small member of the gull family. Its body is built for flying low over the ocean and diving in to catch fish.

White-Bellied Sea Eagle
This huge eagle catches sea snakes, fish and small waterbirds. It also robs other birds of their prey.

Yellow-Eyed Penguin
A rare penguin that lives in New Zealand, this bird nests alone in a burrow.

Glossary

habitat – the natural home of an animal or a plant. Birds live in many different habitats such as deserts, forests, rainforests, grasslands, coastlines and wetlands.

migrate – to move from one country or area to another. Many birds migrate to warmer areas for the winter.

pollution – wastes or poisons that are let out into the air, water or land. Factories and car exhausts both cause a lot of pollution. There are laws for controlling the amount of pollution people make.

preen – to make feathers clean and tidy. Birds preen their feathers with their beaks.

thermal – a rising current of warm air. Birds use thermals to gain height while they fly.

updraft – a current of air that travels upward

wetland – an area of land, such as a tidal flat or swamp, that often contains a lot of water

Index

beaks	4, 6–9, 11–12, 14, 19–20
colonies	15, 19
ducks	13, 20
eagles	6, 21
eggs	4, 6, 16–17
feathers	4–5, 11, 18, 20
feet	6–8, 12, 14, 19–21
flamingos	9
legs	4, 6, 8, 12, 14, 19, 21
pelicans	8, 20
seabirds	5, 8, 13–21
wetlands	10, 19

Discussion Starters

1 Birds live in many different habitats. If you were a bird what habitat would you like to live in? What kind of beak, feet and legs would you have?

2 When people pollute wetlands they destroy the habitat of some waterbirds. What can we do to help keep wetlands free from pollution?

3 When people were building the first aeroplanes they copied the way birds use their wings for flying. Can you think of something that people have copied from waterbirds to help them swim well? What is something else people have copied from birds?